Caribbean Cuisine: Home Cooking Secrets

Alec Q. Gray

All rights reserved.

Copyright © 2024 Alec Q. Gray

Caribbean Cuisine: Home Cooking Secrets : Delicious Island Flavors: Transform Your Kitchen with Caribbean Culinary Techniques

Funny helpful tips:

Stay committed to open dialogue; it prevents misunderstandings.

Avoid taking conflicts to bed; resolving issues ensures peace of mind.

Introduction

This book offers an exploration of traditional Caribbean cooking, providing authentic recipes that are easy to follow and reproduce in any kitchen. The cookbook begins with a comprehensive introduction to cooking Caribbean food, covering cooking methods, tools, and equipment commonly used in Caribbean kitchens. From coal pots to Dutch pots, wooden spoons to mortar and pestle, readers are introduced to the essential tools and techniques that form the foundation of Caribbean cuisine.

The cookbook then dives into the heart of Caribbean cooking with chapters dedicated to appetizers and snacks, chicken dishes, beef and lamb recipes, pork and goat specialties, fish and seafood delights, vegetarian options, and delectable desserts. Each section features a variety of mouthwatering recipes that showcase the vibrant flavors and diverse culinary traditions of the Caribbean islands.

From spicy appetizers to succulent meat dishes, fresh seafood creations to satisfying vegetarian options, this book offers something for every palate and occasion. Whether you're craving the bold flavors of jerk chicken, the comforting richness of oxtail stew, or the refreshing sweetness of coconut desserts, this cookbook provides a wealth of recipes to satisfy your Caribbean food cravings.

With easy-to-follow instructions, helpful cooking tips, and stunning photography that captures the essence of Caribbean cuisine, this book is a must-have cookbook for anyone looking to explore the vibrant and flavorful world of Caribbean cooking.

Whether you're a seasoned cook or a culinary novice, this cookbook will inspire you to bring the taste of the Caribbean into your own kitchen.

Contents

COOKING CARIBBEAN FOOD 1
    Cooking Methods 6
    Tools and equipmentBarbacoa 7
    Coal Pots 8
    Wooden Spoon 8
    Dutch Pot 8
    Jesta Pot 9
    Tava Griddle 9
    Karahi Pot 9
    Mortar and Pestle 9
    Kreng Kreng 10
    Cooking tips for Caribbean Cooking 10

APPETIZERS AND SNACKS 12
    Conch Ceviche 12
    Conch Fritters 14
    Jamaican Patties 16
    Solomon Gundy 18
    Yaniqueque 20
    Pholourie 23
    Breadfruit Fries 26
    Crab Cakes 28
    Mussels in Tomato Dill Sauce 30

CHICKEN 32
    Caribbean Coconut Chicken 32
    Ginger-Tamarind Chicken Thighs 34
    Chicken Fricassee 36
    Chicken Legs Roti 39
    Chicken Pelau 42
    Jerk Chicken 44
    Chicken La Bandera 46

BEEF AND LAMB 51
- Beef Jerk Burger 51
- Antiguan Beef Stew 53
- Pepper Pot Bajan 56
- Pickapeppa and Angostura Lamb 59
- Callaloo Beef 62
- Jamaican Roast Beef 64

PORK AND GOAT 66
- Puerto Rican Plantain Mofongo 66
- Citrus Geera Pork Chops 68
- Coconut Pork Rundown 70
- Bacon and Pumpkin Talkari 72
- Pork Pelau 74
- Jamaican Curry 77
- Goat Scaloppine 80
- Goat Water 82

FISH AND SEAFOOD 84
- Ackee and Saltfish 84
- Dressed Crabs 87
- Flying Fish and Cou-Cou 89
- Caribbean Buljol Butties 92
- Mint-Lime Fish 93
- Fish Escabeche 94
- Shrimp Etouffee 96

VEGETARIAN AND SIDES 98
- Ital Vegetable Stew 98
- Quiche Callaloo 100
- Plantain Tarts 102
- Coconut Rice and Beans 104
- Honied Mac and Cheese 106
- Spiced Cabbage and Corn 108
- Mashed Yam 110
- Bermudan Rice 112

DESSERTS 113
- Jamaican Toto 113
- Caribbean Bread Pudding 115
- Coconut Souffle with Rum 117
- Poached Pawpaw 119
- Hummingbird Cake 120
- Spiced Chocolate Mousse 124
- Salted Caramel Tamarind Ice Cream 126
- Gizzada 128
- Bulla Cakes 130

COOKING CARIBBEAN FOOD

Caribbean cuisine revolves around what is grown on the islands and what can be harvested around them. Caribbean natives eat a lot of seafood and their indigenous fruits and vegetables. Animals raised on the island are also part of their staple diet. Foods in the Caribbean culture are mostly grown and picked by the people there – coming directly from the source – and therefore are normally fresh, natural, and healthy.

What is Caribbean Food?

Conventional Caribbean food is composed of meat and vegetables from the islands. Popular food items include jerk chicken, rice, fish, lamb, plantains, or goat curry. Sodas are common, as are natural fruit juices and shakes. Roti bakeries are common, too, these are made with oxtails, jerk meat, and curry.

Different traditions blended together over the course of time to make up the Caribbean cuisine: African, Latin American, European, Amerindian, Creole, and more. Chicken, pork, and fish are commonly cooked as curries and stews after a long simmer to develop flavors and make sure meat is tender.

Key Ingredients in Caribbean Cooking

Rice and beans are staples in Caribbean kitchens, and so are coconuts, limes, tomatoes, yams, bell peppers, onions, and plantains. Spices and seasonings from the Caribbean include Scotch bonnet pepper, garlic, cilantro, tarragon, and curry, to name only a few.

Here are some of the common ingredients used in Caribbean cuisine that should be stocked in the pantry:

Curry powder

Curry powder as we know it now is a blend of spices that originated from India during the colonial period, and it has since become a staple in Jamaica. However, there is a minor difference between Jamaican and Indian curry powders: the added allspice in Jamaican curry. Local cuisines using this spice are curried dishes such as shrimp, chicken, and goat – which is a lunch staple.

Scotch bonnet pepper

Scotch bonnet peppers are also called "bonney peppers." Others call them Caribbean red peppers. These are some of the most common ingredients in island cooking and are used in jerk dishes as well. Scotch bonnet peppers are intensely hot, in fact, they are listed as one the hottest peppers to exist. The color ranges: they can be yellow, red, or green. Ripe varieties are peach and orange in color. Applications in Caribbean cuisine include dry rubs used for marination, curing, and barbecuing. Don't forget to wear gloves when dealing with this pepper and avoid putting your hands near your eyes.

Allspice

Pimiento and Jamaican peppercorn are the other names associated with allspice. To create allspice, the Pimenta berries are plucked from the fields while unripe and green. They are left to dry under the heat of the sun until brown and will eventually resemble small and round granules similar to peppercorns. These are used whole or ground for cooking and as an ingredient for jerk dishes and are found in both savory and sweet recipes like desserts.

Ginger

Ginger is not native to Caribbean localities, but the tropical and warm climate is suitable for ginger propagation. Aside from in jerk dishes, ginger is used in Caribbean desserts such as cakes and cookies, as well as bringing additional zest and spice to savory dishes.

Cinnamon

Cinnamon, like ginger, is not native to the Caribbean islands; however, it is essential to their cuisine. Cinnamon is not limited to cakes and desserts but is also used in savory dishes such as lamb and chicken and in the cooking of jerk meats. In the use of Caribbean Garam Masala, cinnamon is the primary ingredient.

Nutmeg

The fruit or pod of nutmeg is utilized in Grenada to process jams. As a dessert, these are sliced and cooked with sugar until crystallized to make candy with a pleasing essence. In other parts of the Caribbean, nutmeg is used in addition to drinks such as Barbados rum punch or what they locally call "Bushwacker."

Cloves

Cloves are typically paired with other spices such as nutmeg, cinnamon, and allspice and are notably used in many Caribbean dishes. Another component of Caribbean curry, it's a chemical called eugenol that gives off a strong flavor.

Callaloo

Callaloo is a leafy green plant that is locally abundant in Jamaica, often grown in the gardens of local people. It is a staple in many Jamaican dishes. It can easily be boiled, chopped, seasoned, and accompanied by Scotch bonnet peppers. It is often used in fritters with saltfish. Callaloo is also simply served at breakfast with tomatoes and onions.

Cornmeal

Every Caribbean home has a stock of cornmeal in its pantry. This is a very versatile and cheap ingredient in the islands. Many dishes are born of this raw material, such as cornmeal pudding and porridge. Water is added to the cornmeal, simmered, stirred with various local chopped vegetables and herbs, and paired with heavy Caribbean seasonings. A common dessert is made with nutmeg, raisins, milk, and baked to perfection.

Ackee

Ackee trees and their large red fruit are abundant across the Caribbean islands. However, great care must be taken in the preparation of ackee because some parts of the fruit are poisonous. Store-bought ackee is already prepared and ready to use and may be canned. It looks like scrambled egg and has a bland taste, so it still must be seasoned. Ackee is a breakfast staple in Caribbean cuisine and commonly paired with tomatoes, onion, and Scotch bonnet peppers.

Coconut

Coconut is popularly called the tree of life and gives so much to Caribbean cuisine. Young coconuts are made into jellies. Coconut water is a popular roadside drink. Coconut oil also has been one of the healthiest oils existing in the market and is used in Caribbean cooking. Coconut milk in cans is also available in supermarkets and is a staple in Jamaica.

Tomatoes

Many varieties of tomatoes are grown by the farmers in the Caribbean: Costoluto Florentino, Costoluto Genovese, Carolina Gold, Pink Accordion, Arkansas Traveler, Purple Calabash, Calypso, Heatmaster, Black Krim, Porter, and various cherry tomatoes. Many of these tomato varieties are used soups, rice, stuffed sweet peppers, and their own local pizza recipe.

Lime

Limes utilized in Jamaica are commonly known as "West Indian lime", or as simply as "lime." Lime is not only used as an added ingredient in Caribbean recipes. It has a variety of uses such as in making drinks, washing raw chicken, removing raw or off-odor from fish, and of course, it is a key ingredient in baking key lime pies. This ingredient has definite acidity. It is tart, sour, and sharp. Limes have a distinct aroma, which is one big reason they are abundant in cooking.

Yams

Yams generally look similar to sweet potatoes. The skin is usually rough and rigid. The texture is bark-like and ranges from light brown, tan, or dark brown in color. Although in Caribbean dishes, when cooked, the flesh is white, creamy, or sometimes yellow. The flavor is similar to a regular potato with a hint of nuttiness. This can be steamed, boiled, roasted, fried, scalloped, or creamed.

Plantains

In places such as Cuba, Dominican Republic, and Puerto Rico, plantains are usually mashed and then fried, or made into platanures, tajadas, or tostones. Like potatoes for western cultures, whether boiled, fried, or stuffed, plantains are a popular staple in Caribbean culture.

Rice

In the Caribbean, rice is a staple food crop. The major producers of rice in the islands are Belize, Guyana, and Haiti. Rice is what makes Caribbean cuisine incredibly heavy and high in carbohydrates. It is one of the essential ingredients in their cooking, usually prepared with coconut milk, seasoned with Cajun or Creole spice blends, marinated or dressed generously with sauce or a bit of rum, enhanced with fruit, or combined with legumes and beans.

Beans

Beans are important in the Caribbean islands. Red beans are usually cooked alongside rice and other legumes. The beans are small, oval, slightly nutty, and sweet, and are combined with Latin, Cajun, or Creole seasonings. They are often found in chilis, soups, and stews.

Cooking Methods

Caribbean cuisine is a combination of local and imported flavors, ingredients, and spices, and is prepared using cooking techniques that are influenced by various ethnic groups: Indians, Chinese, Europeans, Africans, and Tainos (the indigenous people of the Caribbean). Now, even though there are modern methods of preparation and cooking, there are still standard customary practices and tools that are unique and traditional for creating authentic dishes.

A Dutch pot is common in most Jamaican households, as well as yabbas – glazed clay pots – now sometimes considered heirlooms more than just cooking tools.

Caribbean traditions have transitioned from wood fires to modern electric stoves and gas ovens.

Tools and equipment

Barbacoa

Barbacoa originated from the Taino, an original Jamaican barbecue, now popularly known as "barbecue." The name literally means "heated sticks." Barbacoa is made from pimiento wood on an elevated platform and is commonly used for cooking jerk pork made from wild pigs. In modern Jamaican kitchens, metal drums are often used and customized for slow-cooking of meats.

Another concept attributed to barbacoa is when a brick oven, about three feet deep, is dug into the ground, where wood is arranged at the bottom and burned until the wood pieces are red hot. Next, a big pot is arranged containing a small amount of liquid, usually water with aromatic herbs or vegetable trimmings. A grill is fixed so the raw meat will not be laid directly on the bottom of the pot. Commonly, lamb or mutton is covered by maguey leaves and transferred to the pot. This will be topped with the animal's stomach, stuffed with a variety of other meats or offal in a mixture of spices, herbs, and chilies. A metal sheet covers the pit and a layer of fresh earth is added. It cooks undisturbed overnight.

Coal Pots

Coal pots are usually about 12 inches in diameter and contain coals to moderate heat and aid in slow cooking. This cooking method promotes rich and deep flavors and sustains more nutrients in food throughout the cooking process. Foods cooked in coal pots have smoked and earthy flavors. Traditional coal pots are one of the earliest cooking methods and food storage containers in the Caribbean region.

Wooden Spoon

Wooden spoons are gentle to the food and do not scratch cookware. These are naturally soft for non-stick pans and cast iron pans and are easy to use because the wood is non-reactive and does not conduct heat. It will not melt or leach harmful chemicals. Thus, nothing compares to the sturdy, smooth grip of a wooden spoon.

Dutch Pot

A Dutch oven is typically a heavy pot made from cast iron, though some are made with stainless steel to be lighter for home cooks. The reason for its heavy bottom is to hold the heat for a long period of time. This is coated with enamel appropriate for cooking at high and low temperatures. (One key factor for this cooking equipment is to allow the pot to cool down sufficiently in-between temperature changes so the enamel won't crack.) These are ideal for slow cooking, such as braises and stews that tend to develop flavor over a long period of time.

Jesta Pot

A jesta pot is also called a digester, or sometimes a roasting pot in western cultures. This cookware is made from enamel-coated cast iron. Similar to the Dutch pot, it is also quite big and can be heavy. Ideally, this is used for cooking pork and beef roasts. This was believed to be used as far back as the 1600s and was invented to be a digester of meat bones; it uses steam heat and pressure to soften and tenderize meat.

Tava Griddle

The Tava griddle is a flat pan for frying. It is most often made from cast iron, carbon steel, or aluminum and may be enameled or have a non-stick surface. This is used to cook roti, leavened and unleavened flatbreads, and pancakes.

Karahi Pot

A karahi pot is a pressed-formed sheet made from steel or iron. This is a wok with steep sides and can be round- or flat-bottomed. A karahi pot is deep and shallow, so it is great for frying sweets and snacks, potatoes, and meats. Examples of dishes cooked here are samosa and fish. Most karahi pots are also used for simmering stews.

Mortar and Pestle

A marble mortar and pestle are commonly used as a type of grinder. It is ideal for crushing whole spices, peeling and mashing garlic, and creating flavorful pastes, sauces, spice blends. Because the marble is nonporous, it will not retain flavor on the surface and is easy to clean.

Kreng Kreng

This is simply a wire basket used as a container to hang over a stove in the kitchen or in a fireplace, suspended in the smoke from the fire. Smoking as a cooking method is traditionally utilized to preserve and cure meats and fish. This dates back to the 19th century where festive hams are processed by curing pork. This is also known as a hangkra.

Cooking tips for Caribbean Cooking

- Use fresh ingredients only. Caribbean cuisine revolves around authentic flavors and deep tastes so avoid settling for canned alternatives. Fresh fruits and vegetables greatly affect the overall flavor of a dish.
- Marinate the meat as directed in the recipes. In utilizing Caribbean sauces, seasoning, and spices such as jerk and the like, the longer the marination, the better, to allow all the flavors to soak in. Overnight marination is ideal.
- Take your time. In Caribbean cooking, slow-cooking for longer times is prevalent. Quick does not mean better – slow cooking brings out the fullness of flavors and allows meat to become tender.
- Use the correct cookware and equipment. As mentioned in the list of cookware, cast iron is common kitchen equipment because these pots are extremely versatile and durable. Being heavy and thick, iron conducts heat better and won't burn the food easily, giving richer stews and flavorful dishes.
- Heat the oil before adding ingredients. Especially in sautéing, to ensure thorough and even cooking, preheat the oil. The concept is, the hotter the pan, the greater the temperature, and the quicker the heat will transfer.

- Do not use too much salt. Caribbean cuisine has its own flavor identity, so don't keep adding unnecessary salt.

APPETIZERS AND SNACKS

Conch Ceviche

A signature dish in the Bahamas, Conch Salad is also one of the most delicious dishes. It is made from diced conch meat, citrus juices, vegetables, and spices.

Serves 4 | Prep. time 40 minutes

Ingredients
1 pound conch meat, fresh, diced
2 tablespoons olive oil
1½ cups tomatoes, fresh, chopped
½ red onion, chopped

1 cup red bell pepper, chopped
1 cup celery, chopped
½ cup orange juice, fresh
¼ cup lime juice, fresh
2 teaspoons Scotch bonnet, chopped
1 teaspoon salt
½ teaspoon black pepper

Directions

1. Wash the conch meat with lemon juice and water. Vinegar can also be used. Drain well.
2. In a large mixing bowl, combine all the ingredients. Blend well and refrigerate for at least 20 minutes.
3. Arrange in small serving bowls and top off with pineapple chunks. Serve when ready.

Nutrition (per serving)

Calories 186, fat 9 g, carbs 12 g, sugar 7 g,
Protein 17 g, sodium 941 mg

Conch Fritters

This is a traditional Bahamas recipe, finger food that is tasty as an hors d'oeuvre.

Serves 8 | Prep. time 1 minutes | Cooking time 4 hours

Ingredients
Oil for deep frying
1 cup all-purpose flour
1 egg
¾ cup milk
½ teaspoon cayenne pepper
1 teaspoon salt
½ teaspoon pepper
1 cup conch meat, diced

1 small onion, finely chopped
1 stalk celery, finely chopped
2 cloves garlic, finely chopped

Directions

1. In a deep pan, heat the oil to 365°F (185°C).
2. In a large mixing bowl, combine the flour, egg, milk, cayenne pepper, and salt and pepper.
3. Add the conch meat, onions, celery, and garlic.
4. Using a slotted spoon, carefully drop the batter into the oil. Fry until golden brown. Drain on paper towels. Serve when ready.

Nutrition (per serving)
Calories 220, fat 14 g, carbs 15 g, sugar 4 g,
Protein 10 g, sodium 209 mg

Jamaican Patties

Delicious beef pastries that are curry-flavored, a favorite snack in the Caribbean islands.

Serves 10 | Prep. time 30 minutes | Cooking time 45 minutes

Ingredients
2 cups all-purpose flour
2 teaspoons curry powder
½ teaspoon salt
½ cup butter
¼ cup shortening
½ cup water
2 tablespoons olive oil
1 pound ground beef

1 sweet onion, chopped
1 teaspoon thyme
½ teaspoon pepper
½ cup beef broth
½ cup breadcrumbs
1 egg, beaten

Directions

1. Preheat the oven to 400°F (204°C).
2. In a large bowl, combine the flour, curry powder, and salt. Cut in the butter and shortening until the mixture is grainy.
3. Gradually add water until the mixture forms a dough. Shape the dough into a log and cut it into 10 equal pieces. Roll each into a 6-inch circle.
4. In a skillet over medium heat, warm the olive oil and brown the beef. Drain any excess fat.
5. Add the onion, thyme, pepper, beef broth, and breadcrumbs. Simmer until all the liquid has been absorbed or evaporated. Remove from heat.
6. Divide the filling onto the pastry circles. Fold them over and press the edges. Brush each patty with a beaten egg.
7. Bake for 30 minutes or until golden brown.

Nutrition (per serving)
Calories 371, fat 25 g, carbs 24 g, sugar 7 g,
Protein 12 g, sodium 477 mg

Solomon Gundy

You'd never guess that Solomon Gundy is not a person but a popular herring pâté dip from Jamaica! It is served on crackers or for a healthier touch on cucumber slices.

*Makes over 1 ½ cup | **Prep. time** 20 minutes | **Cooking time** 10 minutes*

Ingredients
1 pound skinless smoked herring
12 allspice berries
1 small onion, chopped
½ cup white vinegar
1 teaspoon sugar
2 green onions, trimmed and sliced
¼ cup vegetable oil
1 Scotch bonnet pepper, stem removed
½ teaspoon dried thyme

Directions

1. Bring a pot of water to a boil and add herring. Let boil 10 minutes to lower the saltiness of the fish. Drain and let cool.
2. Make sure to remove all bones from the smoked herring.
3. In a saucepan, add the allspice berries, onion, vinegar, and sugar. Cook over medium heat for 2-3 minutes or until the sugar has dissolved. Remove from heat and transfer to a blender or food processor.
4. Add the desalted smoked herring, green onions, vegetable oil, Scotch bonnet pepper, and thyme. and blend until desired consistency. There should still be some texture to the pâté.

5. Serve with crackers or cucumber slices.

Nutrition (per serving – 2 tablespoons)
Calories 150, fat 15 g, carbs 0 g, sugar 0 g,
Protein 4 g, sodium 350 mg

Yaniqueque

Yaniqueques are deep-fried flat bread from the Dominican Republic, originating from the Boca Chica beach area, and are a popular street food or rather beach food!

Makes 8 | Prep. time 15 mins | Cooking time 10 minutes

Ingredients
Dough
2 cups all-purpose flour, plus more for dusting as needed
¼ teaspoon baking powder
¼ teaspoon baking soda
1 teaspoon sea salt
¼ cup lukewarm water

3 tablespoons vegetable oil

Other ingredients
2 cup oil for frying
½ teaspoon coarse sea salt, for sprinkling

Directions

1. Add the flour, baking powder, baking soda, and salt to a mixing bowl. Stir to combine well.
2. Add the water and vegetable oil and mix until a dough ball forms.
3. Transfer the dough ball to a floured working surface and knead the dough Adjust with more water if the dough is too dry or more flour is the dough is too liquid. Do not overwork the dough.
4. Place the dough ball back into the mixing bowl and cover with plastic wrap. Set aside at room temperature for 10-15 minutes.
5. Transfer the dough back to the freshly floured working surface and roll out the dough to about ¾-inch in thickness. Cut the dough into 8 even round pieces with a round empanada cutter or sharp knife.
6. Roll down each piece until very thin almost transparent. Dust often with flour if needed as the dough can get sticky.
7. With a sharp knife, cut some small slits through the dough.
8. Pour the oil in a deep saucepan and warm the oil over medium heat so it reaches 350°F (177 °C). You can also use a deep fryer machine for cooking the yaniqueques.
9. Working in batches so not to crowd the pan, fry the yaniqueques for 2-4 minutes or until golden. Carefully flip over and continue frying until golden brown.

10. With a slotted spoon, remove from oil and transfer to a plate lined with paper towel to absorb excess oil.
11. Dust with coarse sea salt before serving warm.

Nutrition (per serving)
Calories 293, fat 16 g, carbs 32 g, sugar 1 g,
Protein 4 g, sodium 628 mg

Pholourie

Pholouries are tasty and spicy fried dough balls served as appetizers at gathering in Trinidad and Tobago.

*Makes 12-15 | Prep. time 15 minutes | Resting time 1-2 hours
Cooking time 20 minutes*

Ingredients
1 tablespoon parsley
½ Scotch bonnet pepper, chopped
4 cloves garlic, peeled

2 tablespoons fresh cilantro
2 cups all-purpose flour
½ cup split pea flour
2 teaspoons dry yeast
2 teaspoons white sugar
1 teaspoon sea salt
½ teaspoon ground cumin
½ teaspoon turmeric powder
½ teaspoon curry powder
3 tablespoons diced onion
2 green onions, sliced white part only
1 ⅓ cup warm water, more if needed
Vegetable oil for frying

Directions

1. In a blender or small food processor, add the parsley, Scotch bonnet pepper, garlic, onions, and cilantro and blend until smooth.
2. Add the 2 flours, dry yeast, sugar, sea salt, cumin, turmeric, curry, diced onion to a large mixing bowl. Mix until well combined.
3. Add the Scotch bonnet mixture and stir to combine.
4. Slowly add the warm water while stirring until well combined and a dough forms.
5. Place the dough in a warm area away from draught and let rest for 1-2 hours or until the dough has doubled.
6. Add enough oil in a large saucepan to have about 3-inch deep of oil in the pan.
7. Warm the oil over medium heat until it reaches 375°F (191°C) or use a deep fryer.
8. Using an ice cream scooper, drop spoonful of dough carefully in the hot oil. Work in batches and do not overcrowd the saucepan or fryer.

9. Let fry for about 6-7 minutes and then flip over carefully for another 3-4 minutes or until the dough is nicely golden-brown.
10. Transfer the cooked pholouries to a plate lined with paper towels to catch the excess oil.

Nutrition (per serving)
Calories 51, fat 3 g, carbs 5 g, sugar 0 g,
Protein 1 g, sodium 279 mg

Breadfruit Fries

Breadfruit is similar to jackfruit, and in fact, they are relatives. Breadfruit is a staple in the Caribbean and is a very versatile food ingredient.

Serves 4 | Prep. time 20 minutes | Cooking time 20 minutes

Ingredients
1 tablespoon coriander
2 teaspoons paprika
1 teaspoon curry powder
1 teaspoon cumin
½ teaspoon salt
¼ teaspoon black pepper
¼ cup olive oil

1 breadfruit, cleaned, peeled, and sliced

Directions

1. Preheat the oven to 400°F (204°C) and grease a baking sheet.
2. In a bowl, combine coriander, paprika, curry powder, cumin, salt, and pepper. Blend evenly.
3. Pour in olive oil and stir until combined. Add breadfruit slices and toss to coat each piece well. Arrange the pieces on the prepared baking sheet.
4. Bake for 20 minutes. Serve when ready.

Nutrition (per serving)
Calories 189, fat 14 g, carbs 17 g, sugar 6 g,
Protein 1 g, sodium 78 mg

Crab Cakes

Seafood Jamaican style, easy and flavorful. Perfect to start a Carribean meal.

*Serves 4 | Prep. time 20 minutes
Refrigeration time 1 hour | Cooking time 20 minutes*

Ingredients
3 eggs
½ teaspoon salt
½ teaspoon cayenne pepper
1 teaspoon curry powder
1 tablespoon parsley, chopped
2 tablespoons melted butter

2 cups crab meat, drained
¾ cup cashew nuts, chopped
1 cup breadcrumbs
Vegetable oil

Directions

1. In a bowl, beat the eggs with salt, cayenne pepper, curry powder, and parsley. Blend in melted butter and set aside.
2. Shred crab meat using your fingers, remove any shell pieces, and add the meat to the egg mixture.
3. Gently mix in the cashew nuts and breadcrumbs. Refrigerate for 1 hour.
4. Shape the cooled mixture into 10 equal patties.
5. In a skillet over medium heat, fry the prepared patties until golden brown on each side. Serve when ready

Nutrition (per serving)
Calories 306, fat 21 g, carbs 21 g, sugar 4 g,
Protein 10 g, sodium 632 mg

Mussels in Tomato Dill Sauce

Mussels are tasty shellfish that are low in calories and quick to cook.

Serves 8 | Prep. time 10 minutes | Cooking time 35 minutes

Ingredients
2 tablespoons olive oil
1 yellow onion, finely chopped
2 cups tomato, diced
1 cup white wine
½ cup fresh dill, chopped
2 teaspoons red wine vinegar
½ teaspoon oregano, dried
½ teaspoon red pepper flakes
2 pounds mussels, medium, cleaned

Directions

1. In a large non-stick pan, heat the oil over medium heat. Sauté the onions until translucent. Add the tomatoes, white wine, dill, red wine vinegar, and red pepper flakes.
2. Bring to a boil and lower the heat. Simmer until the sauce thickens, about 20 minutes.
3. Add mussels. Cover and cook for about 5 minutes or until the shells are opened. Discard any mussels that don't open.
4. Turn off heat and season with black pepper. Garnish with dill. Serve when ready.

Nutrition (per serving)
Calories 116, fat 3 g, carbs 8 g, sugar 3 g,
Protein 14 g, sodium 331 mg

CHICKEN
Caribbean Coconut Chicken

Delicious, creamy, simple, and easy to make. Can be eaten with any grain or rice, or even with any boiled root crop.

Serves 8 | Prep. time 3½ hours | Cooking time 1 hour

Ingredients
8 pieces chicken drumsticks or thighs, cleaned and skin removed

For the marinade
1 large onion, chopped
3 cloves garlic, chopped

1 teaspoon salt
½ teaspoon black pepper
¼ teaspoon nutmeg
3 whole cloves
1 tablespoon apple cider vinegar
2 tablespoons olive oil

2 tablespoons olive oil
¼ cup parsley, fresh, chopped
1 tablespoon thyme, fresh
1 bay leaf
1 jalapeño pepper, deseeded and minced
1 tablespoon yellow curry powder
1 ¾ cup coconut milk

Directions

1. Place chicken pieces in a large container and add the onion, garlic, salt, pepper, nutmeg, cloves, apple cider vinegar, and olive oil. Cover and marinate for 3 hours.
2. Remove chicken from marinade. Set aside the liquid marinade.
3. In a heavy-bottomed saucepan, heat olive oil over medium heat. Brown the chicken pieces by searing each side. Pour in the chicken marinade and bring it to a boil. Add parsley, thyme, bay leaf, cayenne pepper, curry powder, and coconut milk.
4. Add salt and pepper to taste. Simmer for 40 minutes. Serve when ready.

Nutrition (per serving)
Calories 389, fat 20 g, carbs 6 g, sugar 1 g,
Protein 16 g, sodium 390 mg

Ginger-Tamarind Chicken Thighs

This marinated chicken is best paired with grilled eggplants and shishito peppers.

Serves 6 | Prep. time 20 minutes
Marinating time 4–6 hours | Cooking time 30 minutes

Ingredients
For the tamarind marinade
3 cups water
2 cups tamarind pulp
½ cup fish sauce
1½ cups dark brown sugar
½ cup hot sauce

For the grilled chicken

3 cloves garlic, chopped
1 teaspoon ginger, fresh, grated
1 teaspoon garam masala
½ teaspoon salt
¼ teaspoon red pepper flakes
3 pounds chicken thighs, cleaned and fat removed
¼ cup scallions (for garnish)

Directions

1. Combine the marinade ingredients in a large container with a tight-fitting lid.
2. Toss the chicken with garlic, ginger, garam masala, salt, and red pepper flakes.
3. Add the chicken to the marinade and refrigerate for 4 to 6 hours.
4. Preheat the electric grill to a medium setting. Remove the chicken from the marinade and discard the liquid. Grill the chicken until the internal temperature reaches 165°F (74°C).
5. Allow it to rest before serving. Garnish with scallions. Serve when ready.

Nutrition (per serving)
Calories 182, fat 8 g, carbs 4 g, sugar 4 g,
Protein 21 g, Sodium 447 mg

Chicken Fricassee

This is not a one-pan meal, but it is great if served with rice or potatoes.

Serves 6 | Prep. time 30 minutes | Cooking time 60 minutes

Ingredients
<u>For the chicken thighs</u>
6 chicken thighs, cleaned
2 teaspoons olive oil
1½ teaspoons salt
2 teaspoons paprika
1½ teaspoons cumin
½ teaspoon nutmeg
¼ teaspoon cayenne pepper

For the fricassee
2 tablespoons olive oil
1 white onion, diced
¼ cup celery, chopped
3 cloves garlic, minced
1 bay leaf
1 teaspoon dried thyme
4 ounces cremini mushrooms, sliced
2 ½ tablespoons all-purpose flour
2 cups chicken stock
½ cup sherry wine
¼ cup cooking cream
2 carrots, diced small
1 cup asparagus, trimmed and cut into 1-inch pieces

Directions

1. Drizzle the chicken thighs with the oil and add the seasonings, ensuring to rub them all over the surface.
2. Pour the olive oil into a large skillet over medium heat. Lay the chicken thighs skin side down and allow them to brown for 5 minutes on each side. Transfer the chicken to a plate and discard excess oil from the skillet.
3. Sauté the onion, garlic, celery, bay leaf, thyme, and mushrooms. Cook until mushrooms are soft and then add the flour. Stir for a minute.
4. Pour in the chicken stock and stir constantly until the sauce begins to thicken. Add the wine and season with salt and pepper.
5. Return the chicken to the pan and cover.
6. Allow it to simmer on medium heat for 12 minutes. Remove from the cover and add carrots and asparagus. Cook for 7 more minutes or until carrots is tender.
7. Serve with rice or potatoes.

Nutrition (per serving)
Calories 462, fat 31 g, carbs 14 g, sugar 4 g,
Protein 22 g, sodium 686 mg

Chicken Legs Roti

An amazing chicken meal that might be new to your taste buds and is rich in spices.

Serves 4 | Prep. time 20 minutes
Marinating time 1 hour | Cooking time 60 minutes

Ingredients
2 pounds chicken thighs, cleaned and skins removed, cut into bite-sized pieces

For the chicken marinade
1 teaspoon salt
½ teaspoon black pepper
1 teaspoon garlic, chopped

1 teaspoon thyme, dried
1 teaspoon curry powder
½ teaspoon chicken bouillon powder

For the chicken roti
½ cup vegetable oil
1 red onion, diced
2 teaspoons garlic, chopped
1½ teaspoon cumin
1 teaspoon thyme
2 teaspoons paprika
1 teaspoon allspice
3 tablespoons curry powder
1 teaspoon nutmeg
1 quart chicken broth
1 can chickpeas, drained and rinsed
2 cups potatoes, cubed
1 teaspoon cayenne pepper
1 teaspoon salt

Directions

1. In a large bowl, toss the chicken with salt, pepper, garlic, thyme, curry powder, and bouillon.
2. Mix everything together until well combined. Set aside and marinate in the refrigerator for 1 hour.
3. In a large saucepan over medium heat, pour the oil and sauté the onions, garlic, cumin, thyme, paprika, allspice, curry powder, and nutmeg. Stir until onions are translucent.
4. Add chicken pieces and sauté until lightly browned. Pour in the chicken broth.
5. Finally, add the chickpeas, potatoes, cayenne pepper, and salt. Allow to boil and reduce to simmer until the sauce

thickens about 30 minutes.
6. Season with salt and pepper to taste.

Nutrition (per serving)
Calories 333, fat 24 g, carbs 16 g, sugar 1 g, Protein 12 g, Sodium 580 mg

Chicken Pelau

This is a healthy dish that can be prepared in bulk, stored, and enjoyed as leftovers.

Serves 4 | Prep. time 15 minutes | Cooking time 45 minutes

Ingredients
3 tablespoons brown sugar
2 pounds chicken thighs, cleaned and skin intact, cut into bite-sized pieces
1 can coconut milk
1 ¼ cups chicken broth
1 cup carrots, cubed
1 teaspoon salt

½ teaspoon pepper
1½ cups white rice
1 cup peas

Directions

1. In a heavy-bottomed pot, caramelize the brown sugar, about 3 minutes. Carefully tilt the pan from side to side so as not to burn the sugar. Add the chicken pieces and stir to coat everything.
2. Add the coconut milk, chicken broth, carrots, salt, pepper, and rice. Bring to a boil and reduce to a simmer over medium heat. Cook, covered, for about 25 minutes.
3. Blend in the peas. Continue cooking, covered, for about 5 minutes.
4. Serve when ready.

Nutrition (per serving)
Calories 646, fat 26 g, carbs 74 g, sugar 13 g,
Protein 28 g, sodium 752 mg

Jerk Chicken

This recipe is incredibly flavorful due to a spicy kick and hours of marinating.

Serves 4 | Prep. time 30 minutes
Marinating time 2 hours | Cooking time 30 minutes

Ingredients
For the jerk chicken marinade
1 red onion, chopped
2 scallions, chopped
1 Scotch bonnet pepper, quartered
¼ cup fresh lime juice
1 tablespoon olive oil

1 tablespoon brown sugar
1 tablespoon allspice berries
1 teaspoon cinnamon
1 teaspoon nutmeg
1 teaspoon salt
½ teaspoon thyme, dried

Chicken
2 pounds bone-in chicken, any pieces, cleaned and skins removed

Directions

1. In a blender, process the jerk marinade ingredients until smooth. Arrange the chicken pieces in a baking dish with a cover.
2. Cover chicken with the jerk marinade until evenly coated. Marinate for at least 2 hours.
3. Heat an electric grill or barbecue grill to medium heat.
4. Grill for 6-10 minutes on each side or until the internal temperature of the meat has reached 165°F (74°C).
5. Allow it to rest before serving. Serve when ready.

Nutrition (per serving)
Calories 350, fat 14 g, carbs 9 g, sugar 5 g,
Protein 45 g, Sodium 704 mg

Chicken La Bandera

This is the Dominican Republic's national standard lunch meal, and it is composed of rice, beans, and meat.

Serves 6 | Prep. time 1 hour | Cooking time 2 hours

Ingredients
<u>For the Arroz Blanco</u>
¼ cup vegetable oil
1 teaspoon salt
6 cups water
4 cups rice

<u>For the habichuelas guisadas</u>
2 cups red kidney beans

1 tablespoon olive oil
1 teaspoon oregano dried
1 red bell pepper, chopped
1 red onion, quartered
3 cloves garlic, chopped
1 cup auyama (pumpkin), diced
1 cup tomato sauce
2 sprigs thyme, fresh
1 teaspoon coriander
1 teaspoon salt

For pollo guisado
2 pounds chicken thighs, cut into bite-sized pieces
2 fresh limes cut into halves
1 teaspoon oregano
1 red onion, chopped
1 teaspoon salt
2 cloves garlic, chopped
2 tablespoons water
2 tablespoons oil
1 teaspoon white sugar
2 tomatoes, quartered
2 cubanelle peppers, diced
¼ cup olives, deseeded, halved
1 cup tomato sauce
½ cup chicken stock
1 tablespoon cilantro leaves, chopped
½ teaspoon salt
¼ teaspoon black pepper

For res guisada
2 pounds beef round steak, cut into bite-sized pieces
1 teaspoon salt
½ teaspoon black pepper

1 teaspoon oregano
1 fresh lime juice
3 tablespoons corn oil
3 cups beef stock
1 red onion, sliced
2 tomatoes, quartered
2 bell peppers, diced
3 cloves garlic, chopped
2 cups tomato sauce

For Ensalada Verde
1 beetroot, boiled and sliced
2 tomatoes, sliced
¼ cup cabbage, chopped finely
1 cucumber, diced
1 red bell pepper, cut into thin strips
1 red onion, cut into thin strips
3 tablespoons cooking wine
3 tablespoons olive oil
1 teaspoon salt

Directions
For Arroz Blanco

1. In a saucepan over medium heat, combine the oil, salt, and water. Bring it to a boil.
2. Add the rice and cook, stirring frequently to prevent sticking at the bottom of the pan.
3. When the liquid has evaporated, cover the saucepan, and reduce the heat to low. Cook for 15 minutes and then turn off the heat.

For Habichuelas Guisadas

1. Soak the beans for 12 hours or overnight.

2. Remove from the soaking water and transfer them to Dutch oven with fresh water. Simmer until tender, about 1 hour. Drain.
3. Pour another 4 cups of water over the beans and bring them to a boil again. Lower the heat, and mash and cook until creamy.
4. Add all the spices and seasonings and give it a good stir.

For the *pollo guisado*

1. Season the chicken pieces with lime juice. Add the oregano, red onion, salt, and garlic. Marinate for an hour or two.
2. In a pan, heat the oil over medium, then add the sugar and allow it to brown. Add chicken. Reserve the remaining marinade for the final cooking step. Stir everything until the meat turns brown.
3. Braise by adding 2 tablespoons of water. Cover and simmer over medium heat for 15 minutes. Stir constantly and add a tablespoon of water every now and then to prevent it from burning.
4. Add the vegetables, cover, and simmer.
5. Make the sauce by adding tomato sauce and ½ cup of broth. Simmer over low heat. The vegetables should be soft, and the sauce must be thick. Chicken should be falling off the bones. Add cilantro.
6. Season with salt and pepper.

For the *res guisada*

1. Season beef with salt, pepper, and oregano. Add the lime juice and blend in to coat all the meat pieces. Allow it to marinate, covered, for 30 minutes in the refrigerator.

2. In a heavy-bottomed pan, heat the oil over high and add the meat to brown.
3. Add about ½ cup of water and stir to avoid burning. Repeat until the meat is tender, about 40 minutes.
4. Add the onions, tomatoes, peppers, and garlic, and stir. Cook until vegetables are tender.
5. Add the tomato sauce and a cup of water. Allow the mixture to reduce to produce a light sauce.
6. Season with salt and pepper.

For the ensalada verde

1. Season sliced beets with sugar and lay down the vegetables on a nice platter.
2. To make the vinaigrette, combine the wine and olive oil. Add salt and stir.
3. Serve alongside the dishes in this recipe.

Nutrition (per serving)
Calories 1181, fat 87 g, carbs 206 g, sugar 22 g,
Protein 67 g, Sodium 3335 mg

BEEF AND LAMB

Beef Jerk Burger

A very flavorful Caribbean burger served with fresh mango slaw.

Serves 4 | Prep. time 20 minutes | Cooking time 30 minutes

Ingredients
1 cup coleslaw, prepared
½ ripe mango, julienned
2 teaspoons lime juice
1 pound ground beef
2 tablespoon Caribbean jerk seasoning, prepared
1 red bell pepper, cut in wide slices
½ cup green onions
4 hamburger buns

Directions
1. In a bowl, blend the coleslaw, mango, and lime juice. Cover and refrigerate until ready to serve.
2. Mix the ground beef with the jerk seasoning, gently massaging the beef to distribute the flavor evenly. Shape into 4 round patties.
3. On an electric griller set to medium heat, cook the patties evenly up to an internal temperature of 165°F.
4. Grill the bell peppers for a maximum of 3 minutes or until lightly charred.
5. Serve by assembling the ingredients on burger rolls with the grilled bell peppers, green onions, and mango slaw.

Nutrition (per serving)
Calories 367, fat 11 g, carbs 40 g, sugar 8 g,

Protein 27 g, sodium 547 mg

Antiguan Beef Stew

A stew that can be served as lunch or dinner. Contains lean meat with generous herbs and seasonings to make it flavorful.

Serves 4 | Prep. time 30 minutes | Cooking time 1 hour 30 minutes

Ingredients
1 tablespoon canola oil
1 tablespoon sugar
2 pounds beef sirloin steak, cut into bite-sized cubes

5 tomatoes, chopped
2 medium carrots, diced
2 celery stalks, diced
4 green onions, chopped
1 cup beef stock
¼ cup barbecue sauce, prepared
¼ cup light soy sauce
2 tablespoons steak sauce, prepared
1 tablespoon garlic powder
1 teaspoon thyme, dried
¼ teaspoon allspice powder
¼ teaspoon pepper
⅛ teaspoon cayenne powder

<u>Cornstarch slurry</u>
2 tablespoons cornstarch
2 tablespoons water

Rice or potatoes, for serving

Directions

1. In a Dutch oven, heat the oil over medium heat. Add the sugar and stir until lightly browned about one minute. Add the beef and brown on all sides.
2. Add all the remaining ingredients and bring to a boil. Reduce heat to low and cover. Allow it to simmer until vegetables and meat are tender, about an hour and a half.
3. In a small bowl, mix cornstarch with water and stir into stew. Bring to a boil, cook, and stir until the mixture is thickened.
4. Serve with rice or potatoes.

Nutrition (per serving)
Calories 285, fat 9 g, carbs 18 g, sugar 10 g,

Protein 32 g, sodium 18 mg

Pepper Pot Bajan

This is a holiday stew in Guyana and other parts of the Caribbean. It is cooked over low heat in a dark and thick gravy flavored with cinnamon and brown sugar.

Serves 6 | Prep. time 15 minutes
Marinating time 8 hours+ | Cooking time 2 hours

Ingredients
<u>For the marinated oxtail and beef</u>
2 pounds oxtail, clean and cut into bite-sized pieces
2 pounds beef sirloin, cut into bite-sized pieces
1 teaspoon salt

1 teaspoon pepper
1 teaspoon garlic, minced
1 teaspoon thyme, dried
1 yellow onion, chopped
1 teaspoon beef bouillon powder

For the pepper pot
2 tablespoons brown sugar
3 cloves garlic, chopped
1 red onion, chopped
2 pieces green onion, diced
2 teaspoons thyme
1 Scotch bonnet pepper
1 cup cassareep
3 cups water
1 cinnamon stick, cut in half
1 teaspoon salt
½ teaspoon pepper

Directions

1. In a large bowl, season oxtail and beef with salt, pepper, garlic, thyme, onion, and beef powder. Cover and marinate in the refrigerator overnight.
2. In a Dutch oven pan on medium heat, add sugar and stir to caramelize. Be careful not to let it burn.
3. Add the beef pieces to the pan and brown all sides. Remove from the pan and set aside.
4. Add oxtail pieces and stir continuously to prevent them from burning. Add garlic, onions, thyme, and Scotch bonnet pepper. Cook for 5 minutes.
5. Return the beef to the pot and add the cassareep, water, cinnamon, salt, and pepper. Cover and simmer for 1 hour.

Nutrition (per serving)

Calories 926, fat 48 g, carbs 7 g, sugar 4 g, Protein 112 g, sodium 811 mg

Pickapeppa and Angostura Lamb

Pickapepper is a Jamaican condiment where the main flavors are cane vinegar and cloves, spiced up by onion and thyme.

Serves 6 | Prep. time 30 minutes
Marinating time 2 hours | Cooking time 2 hours

Ingredients
For the pickapeppa sauce
1 cup tomatoes, diced
1 red onion, diced
¼ cup brown sugar
1 cup cane vinegar
1 clove garlic, chopped
½ cup raisins

1 cup mango, diced
1 aji Amarillo chili
1 guajillo chili
1 teaspoon thyme
1 teaspoon ground cloves
1 teaspoon salt
½ teaspoon pepper

For the Angostura lamb
3 pounds lamb chops
1 tablespoon Angostura bitters
3 cloves garlic, chopped
1 teaspoon salt

3 tablespoons oil
3 tablespoons brown sugar
1 tablespoon Worcestershire sauce
1 tablespoon Worcestershire sauce
2 cups beef broth
1 teaspoon cayenne pepper

Directions

1. In a saucepan, combine all ingredients for the pickapeppa sauce. Bring to a simmer and reduce the heat. Cover the pan. Cook for 15 minutes until the chilis and raisins are fully reconstituted. Set aside.
2. Season the lamb chops with Angostura bitters, garlic, and salt. Marinate, covered, in the refrigerator for 2 hours.
3. In another saucepan over medium heat pour oil, add sugar and garlic until caramelized. Stir occasionally. Allow the sugar to brown and add the marinated lamb. Do not stir to caramelize the lamb surfaces for about 3 minutes. Turn the meat upside down to brown on all the sides.

4. When the lamb is nice and brown, pour in the Worcestershire sauce, butter, coconut cream, beef broth, and cayenne pepper. Add pickapeppa sauce to cover.
5. Cook on medium heat until the lamb is tender, about 2 hours. Simmer to reduce the sauce.
6. Serve hot with vegetables or rice.

Nutrition (per serving)
Calories 395, fat 26 g, carbs 14 g, sugar 11 g,
Protein 27 g, sodium 682 mg

Callaloo Beef

Callaloo is a vibrant and fresh mixture of leafy vegetables that are quick and easy to prepare.

Serves 4 | Prep. time 30 minutes | Cooking time 45 minutes

Ingredients
1 bunch fresh callaloo (kale or collard greens)
2 tablespoons olive oil
1 medium onion, chopped
4 cloves garlic, chopped
2 teaspoons thyme, dried
1 pound beef tenderloin, cut in strips
1 tomato, diced
1 Scotch bonnet pepper
1 teaspoon paprika
¼ teaspoon allspice
1 teaspoon salt
½ teaspoon pepper
4 ripe plantains

Directions

1. Remove stems and cut leaves from the callaloo. Soak the leaves in a bowl of cold water for 10 minutes.
2. In a saucepan over medium heat, warm the oil and sauté the onion, garlic, thyme, and beef strips.
3. Add the tomato, Scotch bonnet pepper, paprika, and allspice. Stir in the callaloo leaves.
4. Cook until everything is tender. Add a little water if needed. Season with salt and pepper to taste.
5. Slice plantains in lengthwise pieces and fry in a separate pan with a little bit of oil. Season with salt and pepper. Serve when ready.

Nutrition (per serving)
Calories 67, fat 4 g, carbs 5 g, sugar 2 g,
Protein 2 g, sodium 76 mg

Jamaican Roast Beef

This recipe is cooked in a Dutch oven and baked for 3½ hours, making sure the beef is tender. It is served with red beans and sweet potatoes.

Serves 4 | Prep. time 15 minutes | Cooking time 3½ hours

Ingredients
¼ cup all-purpose flour
1 teaspoon salt
½ teaspoon pepper
2 tablespoons vegetable oil
3 pounds boneless beef chuck roast
1 red onion, chopped
2 cloves garlic, crushed and minced
1 can tomato sauce
1 cup water
½ cup orange marmalade
1 teaspoon cumin
1 teaspoon chili powder
1 cup red beans, cooked, rinsed, and drained
3 sweet potatoes, diced
2 tablespoons cilantro

Directions

1. Preheat the oven to 350°F (177°C).
2. In a large bowl with a cover, blend the flour, salt, and pepper. Add the beef roast and cover, shaking the contents to coat the beef completely.
3. In a Dutch oven, heat the oil over medium heat. Add the beef roast and cook to brown all sides. Remove the beef from the pan and set it aside, covered.

4. Add the onion and garlic to the hot pan. Sauté until the onions are translucent.
5. Deglaze the pan with the tomato sauce, and add the water, orange marmalade, cumin, and chili powder. Cover the Dutch oven with a tight-fitting lid. Bake for 2 hours.
6. Stir in the black beans and potatoes. Cover and bake for 1½ hours or until the meat is tender. Add cilantro. Serve when ready.

Nutrition (per serving)
Calories 890, fat 160 g, carbs 113 g, sugar 53 g,
Protein 64 g, sodium 1040 mg

PORK AND GOAT
Puerto Rican Plantain Mofongo

Plantain Mofongo is a recipe that originated in Puerto Rico and is basically plantain blended with pork rind cracklings and garlic chips. Then finally shaped into a dome or ball.

Serves 4 | Prep. time 10 minutes | Cooking time 20 minutes

Ingredients
Vegetable oil for frying
3 medium-sized plantains, unripe
1½ tablespoons garlic paste
¾ cup pork cracklings or rinds

Directions

1. Pour the oil for frying into a frying pan and heat it up to 350°F (177°C).
2. Cut the plantains into 1-inch chunks and fry for 4 to 6 minutes until golden brown and tender. Remove from oil and drain in paper towels. Allow for it to cool.
3. Once cooled, mash them using the back of a fork and combine with the garlic paste.
4. Blend in pork rinds and mix.
5. Divide the mixture into 4 parts and transfer it to serving plates, forming each in a dome shape.

Nutrition (per serving)
Calories 620, fat 34 g, carbs 57 g, sugar 25 g,
Protein 28 g, sodium 911 mg

Citrus Geera Pork Chops

This pork dish is packed with spicy pepper and flavorful cumin.

Serves 6 | Prep. time 30 minutes | Cooking time 60 minutes

Ingredients
4 pounds pork chops
1 fresh lime, juiced
1½ tablespoons ground cumin
1 tablespoon green Caribbean seasoning
½ teaspoon salt
¼ teaspoon black pepper
2 tablespoons corn oil
½ teaspoon cumin seeds
2 scallions, chopped
4 cloves garlic, crushed
8 chili peppers
2 pieces pimiento peppers, diced
2 tablespoons cilantro, fresh, chopped
1 tablespoon parsley, fresh, chopped
1¼ cups pork broth

Directions

1. Wash the pork with fresh lime juice and water. Place in a colander to drain and transfer it to a large bowl.
2. Season the pork meat with cumin powder, green Caribbean seasoning, salt, and pepper. Blend everything together.
3. In a saucepan over medium heat, heat the vegetable oil and blend in cumin seeds. Lower the heat and allow this to cook for about 3 minutes to extract the flavor.
4. Add scallions, garlic, chili peppers, pimiento peppers, garlic, cilantro, and parsley.

5. Increase the heat to medium-high and add the pork. Stir everything well to combine all the flavors. Do not cover. Cook until the pork is seared.
6. Allow the mixture to cook until the natural meat juices come out. Heat must be on medium-high. Cook for 10 minutes, stirring constantly.
7. Add the pork broth and bring to a boil. Once done, reduce the heat to a low and allow it to simmer.
8. Continue to simmer on low for 35 minutes or until the liquid is greatly reduced.

Nutrition (per serving)
Calories 388, fat 14 g, carbs 7 g, sugar 1 g,
Protein 56 g, sodium 729 mg

Coconut Pork Rundown

A flavorful pork stew cooked in coconut milk, onions, tomato, garlic, and seasoning. Best served with boiled plantains.

Serves 4 | Prep. time 15 minutes | Cooking time 30 minutes

Ingredients
2 tablespoons canola oil
2 pounds pork sirloin, cut into bite-sized pieces
1 yellow onion, diced
1 bay leaf
1 teaspoon thyme
1 Scotch bonnet pepper
2 tomatoes, chopped
1 teaspoon paprika
1 teaspoon Creole seasoning

1 can coconut milk
½ teaspoon salt
1 teaspoon black pepper
1 tablespoon garlic powder
2 tablespoons parsley, chopped

Directions

1. In a large skillet, heat the oil over medium heat. Add the pork and cook until it is browned on all sides.
2. Add the onion, bay leaf, thyme, and Scotch bonnet pepper. Stir everything together.
3. Add tomatoes, paprika, Creole seasoning, coconut milk, salt, pepper, garlic powder, and parsley.
4. Bring the mixture to a boil and simmer for about 5 minutes. Simmer until the sauce is thick and adjust seasonings as needed.
5. Remove from heat, remove the bay leaf, and serve.

Nutrition (per serving)
Calories 200, fat 7 g, carbs 3 g, sugar 1 g,
Protein 28 g, sodium 90 mg

Bacon and Pumpkin Talkari

Sautéed cubes of pumpkin are then steamed and mashed to a paste-like consistency. This talkari is intensified with roasted ground geera.

Serves 8 | Prep. time 15 minutes | Cooking time 1 hour

Ingredients
½ cup vegetable oil
1 yellow onion, thinly sliced
10 cloves garlic, chopped
2 pounds pumpkin, peeled and cut into small cubes
1 teaspoon roasted geera (cumin)
2 teaspoons salt
1 tablespoon brown sugar

½ teaspoon cayenne pepper

Directions

1. In a heavy-bottomed pan or Dutch oven, heat the oil over medium heat and add the onion. Cook until lightly browned.
2. Add the garlic and cook for another minute. Add the pumpkin and stir to blend evenly. Add salt, sugar, and cayenne, and reduce heat to low. Cook until the pumpkin is tender. Stir occasionally to prevent burning.
3. Once it is soft, mash the pumpkin until it achieves a smooth, paste-like texture. Add the cumin.
4. Serve with rice or pita bread. Serve when ready.

Nutrition (per serving)

Calories 139, fat 11 g, carbs 11 g, sugar 5 g,
Protein 2 g, sodium 294 mg

Pork Pelau

Pelau is an iconic recipe from Trinidad, usually cooked on weekends where family or friends hang out. This dish is made from pork, chicken, or pigeon peas with rice, coconut milk, and herbs.

Serves 6 | Prep. time 20 minutes | Cooking time 1 hour

Ingredients
2 tablespoons green seasoning
2 teaspoons garlic, chopped
1 tablespoon soy sauce
1 tablespoon tomato ketchup
1 teaspoon salt
½ teaspoon black pepper
3 pounds pork shoulder, cut into 1-inch cubes

2 tablespoons corn oil
3 tablespoons brown sugar
2 cups cooked rice
1 yellow onion, chopped
½ cup red bell pepper, chopped
2 cups pigeon peas
2 carrots, peeled and diced
2 cups coconut milk
2 cups pork stock
1 Scotch bonnet pepper, minced
½ cup green onions, sliced

Directions

1. In a large bowl, combine the green seasoning, garlic, soy sauce, ketchup, and salt and pepper. Mix well and add the pork.
2. Mix to coat meat evenly. Cover and refrigerate for an hour.
3. In a large cooking pot over medium heat, warm the oil. Add the sugar and allow it to brown.
4. Drain the marinade and add the pork to the pan. Stir to coat with the burned sugar and cook for 10 minutes.
5. Add the cooked rice and stir.
6. Next, blend in the onion, red bell pepper, pigeon peas, and carrots. Add the coconut milk and the pork stock. Season with salt and pepper. Add the Scotch bonnet pepper and cover the pan.
7. Allow the mixture to boil and partially cover to simmer for 10 minutes.
8. Cover again fully and simmer for 30 minutes.
9. Garnish with green onions and fold them into the pelau. Adjust seasonings as needed. Serve when ready.

Nutrition (per serving)

Calories 692, fat 31 g, carbs 44 g, sugar 10 g,
Protein 63 g, sodium 2240 mg

Jamaican Curry

A melt-in-your-mouth spiced pork curry bursting with full Caribbean flavor.

Serves 6 | Prep. time 20 minutes | Cooking time 3½ hours

Ingredients
Canola oil for frying
2 pounds pork shoulder, cut into 1-inch pieces
2 yellow onions, chopped finely
2 teaspoons allspice
3 tablespoons curry powder
1 tablespoon paprika
1 tablespoon ground coriander ground

1 tablespoon celery salt
1 tablespoon garlic powder
1 tablespoon thyme leaves
½ cup pumpkin, sliced
¼ teaspoon black pepper
6 cloves garlic, thinly sliced
1 Scotch bonnet chili, minced
4 tomatoes, chopped
4 pieces spring onions, chopped

For the rice and beans
¼ cup butter
2 cups long-grain rice
2 tablespoons thyme
1 can kidney beans, drained and rinsed
1½ cups coconut milk
2 cups cold water

Directions

1. In a large pan, Dutch oven, or Jesta pot, heat oil enough to cover the bottom over medium heat. Cook onions until translucent.
2. Add the pork and all the spices. Stir everything together to coat the meat evenly. Mix in garlic, chili, pumpkin, tomatoes, and spring onions. Stir again.
3. Pour in a gallon of cold water and cover the pan. Allow the mixture to boil and then reduce the heat to low to simmer. Cook for 3 hours but stir frequently.
4. While the meat is cooking, prepare the rice and beans. In a pan with a cover, heat the butter over medium heat and add the rice, thyme, and beans. Mix everything together and ensure that the rice is evenly coated.

5. Add the coconut milk and cold water. Stir and cover. Adjust the heat to low and allow to cook for 20 minutes.
6. Using a wooden spoon, fluff the rice. Serve both together!

Nutrition (per serving)
Calories 677, fat 28 g, carbs 59 g, sugar 7 g,
Protein 42 g, sodium 586 mg

Goat Scaloppine

This is the contemporary Caribbean version of traditional scaloppine.

Serves 4 | Prep. time 15 minutes | Cooking time 30 minutes

Ingredients
4 pieces goat scallopini
½ cup all-purpose flour
1 egg
3 tablespoons milk
1 cup panko breadcrumbs
2 tablespoons olive oil
2 tablespoons butter
3 cups arugula
1 cup tomatoes
1 lemon
2 tablespoons canola oil
¼ cup grated Parmesan cheese

Directions

1. Dredge the goat pieces in flour. In a small bowl, beat the egg and add the milk. Dip the dredged goat pieces in it and finally coat with breadcrumbs.
2. Place the meat in the refrigerator, covered, for about an hour.
3. In a large frying pan, heat the oil and butter over medium heat to sizzle. Cook the scallopine until lightly browned on each side or about 2 minutes per side.
4. Remove goat from the pan and allow it to cool. Assemble the arugula and tomatoes and add the lemon juice and olive oil. Arrange the goat scaloppine on top.

5. Season with salt and pepper and garnish generously with Parmesan cheese. Serve when ready.

Nutrition (per serving)
Calories 340, fat 22 g, carbs 32 g, sugar 3 g,
Protein 7 g, Sodium 260 mg

Goat Water

Goat meat stew is a traditional dish in most of the Caribbean countries.

Serves 6 | Prep. time 30 minutes | Cooking time 2 hours 45 minutes

Ingredients
1 juice of a lemon
2 pounds goat meat, cut into small bite-sized pieces
1 tablespoon canola oil
1 tablespoon brown sugar
2 teaspoons ground cloves
1 teaspoon allspice
2 teaspoons mace
1 teaspoon thyme
6 cloves garlic
1 Scotch bonnet pepper, diced
1 stalk celery, diced
¼ cup green bell pepper, diced
1 red onion, diced
1 teaspoon salt
3 pieces bay leaves
1 teaspoon cornstarch
2 tablespoons rum

Directions

1. Wash the goat meat with lemon juice and water. Pat it dry with a paper towel and set aside.
2. In a large saucepan, heat the oil over medium-high heat and add sugar. Cook until it caramelizes. Add the goat meat and stir to coat all sides with the caramel sauce. Add all the spices and pour in a gallon of water.

3. Cover the pan and bring it to a boil. Reduce the heat and simmer for about 2 ½ hours. The meat should be tender.
4. Mix the starch with water and add it to the pot. Simmer for another 10 minutes to thicken. Stir in the rum. Serve when ready.

Nutrition (per serving)
Calories 228, fat 6 g, carbs 7 g, sugar 0 g,
Protein 35 g, sodium 470 mg

FISH AND SEAFOOD
Ackee and Saltfish

Ackee and saltfish is the national dish of Jamaica. It's the perfect dish for a large breakfast, lunch, or brunch with friends. Ackee is a fruit that grows in Jamaica and when it's cooked, it looks like scrambled eggs, but the taste is creamy and nutty.

*Serves 4 | Prep. time 15 minutes | Resting time 4 hours
Cooking time 12-15 minutes*

Ingredients
½ pound boneless salted codfish

¼ cup vegetable oil, more if needed
4 cloves garlic, minced
1 sprig fresh thyme
2 onions, sliced
4 green onions, sliced
½ small green bell peppers, trimmed and sliced
½ small red bell peppers, trimmed and sliced
½ Scotch bonnet pepper, seed removed and minced
1 (20-ounce) can ackee
½ teaspoon paprika
½ teaspoon black pepper

Directions

1. Rinse the salted cod under running water and place in a large bowl. Cover with cold water and place in the refrigerator for 4 hours. Change water at least once.
2. After 4 hours, drain the water and rinse the fish one least time. Set aside.
3. Add the oil to a skillet and warm over medium heat. Add the onions and fry for 2 minutes. Add the garlic, thyme sprig, and Scotch bonnet pepper and continue cooking for 3 minutes
4. Reduce heat to medium-low and add the fish. Stir-fry for 5-6 minutes.
5. Place the ackee in a strainer and rinse under cold water. Stir in the ackee and continue cooking for about 3 minutes, until warmed through.
6. Season with the paprika and black pepper. Stir to combine. Taste and adjust seasoning if needed.
7. Remove the thyme sprig before serving warm.

Nutrition (per serving)
Calories 430, fat 10 g, carbs 64 g, sugar 21 g,

Protein 21 g, sodium 1004 mg

Dressed Crabs

This recipe shows how to properly pick crab meat.

Serves 4 | Prep. time 30 minutes

Ingredients
4 cooked crabs
2 cups breadcrumbs
1 teaspoon salt
½ teaspoon cayenne pepper
3 lemons, juiced
2 tablespoons parsley, chopped
¼ cup mayonnaise

Directions

1. Arrange the crab pieces in a single layer with back sides down. Twist off the claws and legs. Set those aside.
2. Use the palms to push down on the crabs. Where the body meets the back of the shell, pull upwards to separate the crab body from the shell in one piece.
3. Discard the crab gills around the main body and inside the shell. Scoop out the brown meat from the crab and transfer it into a bowl. Using a knife or a cleaver, cut the main body in half.
4. Using a skewer, pick out the white meat from the crab's claws and legs and place it in a separate bowl. There will be pieces that are difficult to remove; just be patient.
5. Scrape the shells clean.
6. Add breadcrumbs to the brown crabmeat to make it stiff. Season with salt, pepper, cayenne, and lemon juice.
7. Divide the white meat into the shells and add the brown meat mixture on top. Garnish with parsley and serve with mayonnaise and lemon wedges on the side. Serve when ready.

Nutrition (per serving)
Calories 215, fat 7 g, carbs 9 g, sugar 0 g,
Protein 27 g, sodium 190 mg

Flying Fish and Cou-Cou

This is a national dish of Barbados. It is cooked in a creole sauce and served with cornmeal and okra.

Serves 6 | Prep. time 30 minutes | Cooking time 50 minutes

Ingredients
For the flying fish
12 pieces flying fish
2 fresh limes, juiced
2 tablespoons salt
1 cup water

1 cup all-purpose flour
3 eggs, beaten
1 cup panko breadcrumbs
Canola oil for frying

<u>For the Creole sauce</u>
3 tablespoons olive oil
2 onions, sliced
2 red bell peppers, sliced
2 cloves garlic, chopped
1 tablespoon thyme
1 can crushed tomatoes
1 teaspoon white sugar
1 tablespoon vinegar
½ cup fish stock
¼ cup parsley, chopped
1 teaspoon salt

<u>For the Cou-cou</u>
3 cups boiling water
1 teaspoon salt
12 pieces okra, sliced into ½ inch pieces
2 cups yellow cornmeal
2 cups cold water
2 tablespoons olive oil

Directions

1. For the flying fish, in a bowl with a cover, marinate the fish with lime juice, salt, and water for 15 minutes. Once done, drain the marinade and dry fish the fillets with a paper towel.
2. Coat each piece of fish with flour and dip in the egg mixture, and finally, coat well with the breadcrumbs.

3. Heat a few inches of canola oil in a heavy pot to 350°F (177°C) and fry the fish until golden brown. Set aside.
4. Prepare the Creole sauce. In a skillet, heat the oil and sauté the onions, red bell pepper, and garlic over medium heat.
5. Add thyme, tomatoes, sugar, vinegar, and fish stock. Cover the pan and allow it to simmer for 15 to 20 minutes.
6. Add parsley and salt. Stir and turn off the heat.
7. Meanwhile, make the Cou-cou. To a pot with 3 cups of boiling water, add salt, and toss in the okra slices. Allow to boil for 10 minutes and turn off the heat. Remove the okra from the boiling water and retain the water.
8. Add the cornmeal to the 2 cups of cold water. Let it sit for a few minutes.
9. When the okra has been removed from the hot water, set half of it aside.
10. To the hot water in the pot, whisk the soaked cornmeal. Cook it and stir constantly until it thickens. Add the okra.
11. As the water is absorbed, add more from the water that was set aside.
12. Continue until it begins to solidify and pull away from the edges of the pot.
13. Grease a bowl with the oil and transfer the Cou-cou to it. Let it set and then turn it out onto a plate.
14. Serve with fish and Creole sauce.

Nutrition (per serving)
Calories 274, fat 10 g, carbs 42 g, sugar 2 g,
Protein 5 g, sodium 501 mg

Caribbean Buljol Butties

A favorite Sunday morning breakfast in Trinidad.

Serves 4 | Prep. time 20 minutes | Cooking time 20 minutes

Ingredients
¼ cup canola oil
2 red onions, chopped
3 tomatoes, chopped
2 red bell peppers, chopped
1 pound cod fish, salted, flaked
1 tablespoon fresh lime juice
1 teaspoon red pepper flakes
6 romaine lettuce leaves
1 avocado, sliced

Directions

1. In a large frying pan, heat the oil and sauté the onions, tomatoes, and peppers over medium heat.
2. Mix in the flaked cod, lime juice, and red pepper flakes. Cook over low heat until the liquids are reduced.
3. Arrange the mixture in a serving bowl with lettuce and avocados on the side. Serve when ready.

Nutrition (per serving)
Calories 431, fat 23 g, carbs 18 g, sugar 6 g,
Protein 40 g, sodium 400 mg

Mint-Lime Fish

For an additional kick, add red pepper flakes for the fish coating.

Serves 6 | Prep. time 10 minutes | Cooking time 120 minutes

Ingredients
¼ cup Italian dressing or mayonnaise
6 (6-ounce) cod fillets with skin
¼ cup brown sugar
1 teaspoon cumin
¼ cup fresh lime juice
1 cup fresh orange juice
¼ cup cilantro, chopped
2 tablespoons mint leaves, chopped

Directions

1. In a large frying pan, heat the dressing over medium heat.
2. Pat the fish dry and sprinkle both sides with brown sugar and cumin. Put the fish in the frying pan skin side down. Cook for 5 minutes on each side (or until cooked through). Remove it from the pan and cover to keep warm.
3. In the skillet, combine the lime and orange juice and cook on medium heat. Stir frequently. Turn off heat, add mint and cilantro. Spoon this over the fish.

Nutrition (per serving)
Calories 150, fat 1.5 g, carbs 13 g, sugar 11 g,
Protein 21 g, sodium 230 mg

Fish Escabeche

Spicy, tarty, and slightly sweet sauce poured over a red snapper fish.

Serves 4 | Prep. time 15 minutes | Cooking time 30 minutes

Ingredients
¼ cup canola oil
2 pounds red snapper, cleaned and descaled
1 bay leaf
2 cloves garlic, chopped
1 teaspoon fresh ginger, grated
1 yellow onion, sliced
1 carrot, julienned
1 red bell pepper, sliced

1 yellow bell pepper, sliced
1 Scotch bonnet pepper, minced
1 teaspoon salt
½ teaspoon black pepper
1 tablespoon thyme
½ teaspoon allspice
1 lime, juiced
1 tablespoon brown sugar
1 cup red wine vinegar
Thyme sprigs for garnish

Directions

1. In a large frying pan over medium heat, warm the oil and cook fish, skin side down. Cook for about 7 minutes on each side or until crispy on both sides. Transfer to a plate with a paper towel to remove excess oil.
2. To the same frying pan, add the bay leaf, garlic, ginger, onion, carrot, bell peppers, and Scotch bonnet pepper.
3. Season with salt, pepper, thyme, allspice, lime juice, and brown sugar. Bring it to a simmer and cook for about 3 minutes. Stir in the vinegar
4. Serve fish on a plate with sauce and garnish with thyme sprigs.

Nutrition (per serving)
Calories 317, fat 18 g, carbs 11 g, sugar 6 g,
Protein 24 g, sodium 101 mg

Shrimp Etouffee

Rich creole shrimp of the Caribbean.

Serves 4 | Prep. time 15 minutes | Cooking time 45 minutes

Ingredients
1 pound shrimp, deveined and peeled, set aside shrimp shells
4 tablespoons butter, divided
1 yellow onion, diced
½ cup celery, chopped
2 cloves garlic, chopped
1 cup green bell pepper, chopped
2 tablespoons soybean oil
¼ cup all-purpose flour

1 teaspoon thyme
1 bay leaf
1 cup tomatoes, chopped
1 tablespoon Creole seasoning
1 teaspoon paprika
2 cups fish broth
3 tablespoons parsley, chopped
2 green onions, chopped

Directions

1. Make the shrimp stock. In a saucepan over medium heat, melt 2 tablespoons of butter and add the shrimp shells and the scraps and peelings from the onion, celery, and garlic. Sauté and stir for 3 to 4 minutes. Add a gallon of water to it and bring to a boil. Remove the pot from the heat and strain out the scraps and shells, reserving the stock.
2. For the etouffee, in a heavy-bottomed saucepan, melt the remaining butter and add the oil and flour. Mix until smooth.
3. Add the onion, celery, garlic, and green bell pepper and mix well. Add the shrimp, thyme, and bay leaf. Mix well.
4. Blend in the tomatoes, Creole seasoning, and paprika. Pour about 2 cups of shrimp stock and bring to a boil and simmer for 5 minutes, or until the shrimp is cooked.
5. Adjust salt and pepper, stir in the parsley and green onions. Serve when ready!

Nutrition (per serving)
Calories 300, fat 15 g, carbs 13 g, sugar 2 g,
Protein 27 g, Sodium 215 mg

VEGETARIAN AND SIDES

Ital Vegetable Stew

Ital stew originated from Jamaica during the Rastafarian movement. Traditionally, this does not contain meat or any processed food. It only contains vegetables, aromatics, and coconut milk.

Serves 4 | Prep. time 20 minutes | Cooking time 50 minutes

Ingredients
1 tablespoon vegetable oil
1 yellow onion, chopped
5 cloves garlic, chopped
2 green onions, chopped

2 stalks celery, chopped
1 teaspoon thyme
1 teaspoon rosemary
½ teaspoon marjoram
1½ teaspoons Italian seasoning
6 allspice berries
¼ cup liquid aminos
1 tablespoon tomato paste
2 russet potatoes, cut into cubes
2 carrots, sliced in thin rounds
½ cabbage, chopped
1 can coconut milk
4 cups water
1 cup soy curls
1 teaspoon salt
½ teaspoon cayenne pepper

Directions

1. In a Dutch oven on medium heat, warm the oil and sauté the onions until soft and translucent.
2. Add the garlic, green onions, and the rest of the aromatics. Stir frequently until fragrant, about 2 minutes.
3. Pour in the liquid aminos, tomato paste, potatoes, carrots, and cabbage. Blend everything well and cook for about 2 minutes.
4. Stir in coconut milk and water. Bring to a boil and simmer for 30 minutes or until the mixture thickens. (Add soy curls halfway through.)
5. Season with salt and cayenne pepper. Serve!

Nutrition (per serving)
Calories 308, fat 17 g, carbs 35 g, sugar 4 g,
Protein 3 g, Sodium 479 mg

Quiche Callaloo

This quiche can be served with akee, vegan rundown, dumplings, or breadfruit.

Serves 6 | Prep. time 10 minutes | Cooking time 50 minutes

Ingredients
1 (12-inch) flour tortilla
¼ cup onion, finely chopped
2 cups callaloo, washed
3 eggs
3 egg whites
1 cup mozzarella cheese, grated
¼ cup Parmesan cheese, grated

½ cup whole milk
½ teaspoon salt
¼ teaspoon black pepper

Directions

1. Preheat the oven to 375°F (191°C). Grease a 9-inch pie plate with a non-stick cooking spray.
2. Arrange the tortilla wrap in the pie plate and press the edges firmly.
3. In a skillet over medium heat, add the oil and sauté the onions for three minutes or until tender and translucent.
4. Add callaloo and cook until just until wilted, stirring often. Turn off the heat and set it aside.
5. In a bowl, blend the eggs, egg whites, cheeses, milk, and salt and pepper. Use a wire whisk to properly blend ingredients until fluffy.
6. Add the callaloo mixture to the egg mixture and blend together. Pour this into the pie plate.
7. Bake for 40 minutes or until the top is golden brown. Remove from the oven and rest it on a wire rack before serving.

Note: if you cannot find Callaloo, you can substitute with baby spinach or even collard greens.

Nutrition (per serving)
Calories 377, fat 16, carbs 38g, sugar 7 g,
Protein 20 g, Sodium 989 mg

Plantain Tarts

An easy-to-make Jamaican recipe using ripe plantains as a filling.

Serves 8 | Prep. time 30 minutes
Chilling time 3 hours | Cooking time 50 minutes

Ingredients
For the pastry dough
2 cups all-purpose flour
½ teaspoon salt
¼ cup butter, unsalted cut into ½ inch cubes
¼ cup shortening, chilled and cubed
1 egg, beaten
1 tablespoon cold water

For the filling

3 plantains, very ripe
¼ cup white sugar
1 teaspoon vanilla extract
1 teaspoon nutmeg.
1 egg white, beaten

Directions

1. In a bowl, prepare the pastry dough. Mix the flour and salt in a bowl. Cut in the butter and shortening until blended. The mixture should be grainy. Add eggs and water and blend into the flour mixture until a dough forms. Knead for a minute or two and wrap in a cling wrap. Chill for 3 hours.
2. While waiting for the dough to chill, pour water in a small pan or double boiler, or steamer and bring to a simmer. Steam the plantains for 10 minutes or adjust based on the ripeness. Once soft, transfer to a bowl and mash the plantain together with the sugar, vanilla, and nutmeg. Set aside and allow to cool.
3. Preheat the oven to 350°F (177°C). Roll out the dough to ¼-inch thickness. Use a 5-inch round cookie cutter to cut circles.
4. Place a spoonful of the banana mixture in the center of each dough circle and fold the dough in half. Seal the edges using the tines of a fork and place the tarts on a baking sheet. Brush the tops with egg white and sprinkle with sugar.
5. Bake for 30 minutes or just until golden brown. Allow the tarts to cool before serving.

Nutrition (per serving)
Calories 106, fat 4 g, carbs 17 g, sugar 6 g,
Protein 2 g, sodium 113 mg

Coconut Rice and Beans

A Caribbean staple that is easy and flavorful and brings a tropical flair to any meal.

Serves 6 | Prep. time 15 minutes | Cooking time 35 minutes

Ingredients
2 tablespoons butter
½ yellow onion, diced
1 clove garlic, chopped
1 cup dry white rice
1 bay leaf
1 teaspoon thyme
½ teaspoon black pepper
1 cup water

½ cup coconut milk, canned
½ cup kidney beans, cooked
½ teaspoon salt

Directions

1. Heat the butter in a saucepan over medium heat. Sauté the onion and garlic.
2. Add the rice, bay leaf, thyme, pepper, water, and coconut milk. Bring this to a boil and simmer for 10 minutes, covered.
3. Add the cooked beans and continue to cook until all the liquid has evaporated and absorbed by the rice, about 10 minutes. Remove the bay leaf and season with salt. Serve when ready.

Nutrition (per serving)
Calories 136, fat 23 g, carbs 89 g, sugar 1 g,
Protein 12 g, sodium 550 mg

Honied Mac and Cheese

Trinidad's macaroni pie is a comfort food classic.

Serves 8 | Prep. time 15 minutes | Cooking time 50 minutes

Ingredients
2 cups elbow macaroni, dry
1 tablespoon salted butter
¼ cup red onion, finely chopped
2 eggs
3 cups evaporated milk
½ teaspoon black pepper
1 teaspoon garlic powder
1½ teaspoons mustard powder
½ teaspoon thyme

½ teaspoon cayenne pepper
3½ cups grated sharp cheddar cheese, sharp

Directions

1. Preheat the oven to 350°F (177°C). Grease a 9x11 baking dish.
2. Cook the macaroni according to the package directions. Drain and place the noodles in the prepared baking dish.
3. In a pan, melt the butter and sauté the onions until caramelized. Pour this over the cooked macaroni.
4. Beat the eggs in a bowl, and add the milk, pepper, garlic powder, dry mustard, thyme, and cayenne pepper. Stir everything together.
5. Pour this egg mixture into the macaroni and toss everything until well combined. Fold in the grated cheese.
6. Bake for 40 minutes until the top is golden brown. Rest the dish before serving.

Nutrition (per serving)
Calories 484, fat 26 g, carbs 36 g, sugar 10 g,
Protein 24 g, sodium 508 mg

Spiced Cabbage and Corn

This pretty side dish has a nice balance of sweet and spicy kick.

Serves 6 | Prep. time 20 minutes | Cooking time 30 minutes

Ingredients
2 tablespoons olive oil
1 red onion, thinly sliced
½ green bell pepper, diced
1 green onion, sliced
2 sprigs thyme
1 Scotch bonnet pepper, whole
1 teaspoon salt
1 medium head of cabbage, shredded
1 cup corn kernels

1 carrot, peeled and sliced
¼ cup white vinegar
2 tablespoons white sugar

Directions

1. In a skillet over medium heat, add the oil and sauté the onion, green bell pepper, and green onion until all vegetables are softened. Add thyme, Scotch bonnet pepper, and salt.
2. Add the shredded cabbage, corn, and carrots to the skillet and stir-fry. Cook until cabbage is tender, stirring frequently. Cover the pan and simmer for 10 minutes.
3. Pour in the vinegar and sugar. Stir to combine for about 3 minutes.
4. Remove the Scotch bonnet pepper before serving.

Nutrition (per serving)
Calories 121, fat 5 g, carbs 19 g, sugar 12 g,
Protein 3 g, sodium 437 mg

Mashed Yam

A nice alternative to mashed potatoes, smooth and creamy.

Serves 4 | Prep. time 15 minutes | Cooking time 30 minutes

Ingredients
6 cloves garlic, mashed
½ red bell pepper, chopped
½ green bell pepper, chopped
2 tablespoons coconut oil, melted
1 pound yams, peeled and cubed
1 cup coconut milk
2 tablespoons butter
¼ teaspoon salt
½ teaspoon black pepper

Directions

1. Preheat the oven to 400°F (204°C). Line a baking tray with parchment and arrange the garlic and bell pepper on it. Drizzle with coconut oil and roast for 15 minutes. Remove from the oven and set aside.
2. Place the yam cubes in a saucepan with water to cover. Boil until tender, about 15 minutes. Drain and mash with the coconut milk until smooth.
3. Mix in the butter and salt.
4. Squeeze the garlic pulp from the roasted garlic and add salt and black pepper.
5. Finally, when the roasted peppers are cool, remove the skins. Add the roasted peppers to the yam mixture and fold them in.

Nutrition (per serving)
Calories 301, fat 17 g, carbs 36 g, sugar 2 g,
Protein 3 g, sodium 1137 mg

Bermudan Rice

Rice seasoned with bacon and aromatic spices, not vegetarian but a great side to any island-style meal.

Serves 6 | Prep. time 30 minutes | Cooking time 45 minutes

Ingredients
6 slices bacon, chopped
1 onion, chopped
1 red bell pepper, chopped
2 cups tomatoes, chopped
¼ cup tomato paste
1½ cups rice
Salt and pepper to taste
2 cups water or chicken stock

Directions

1. Preheat the oven to 350°F (177°C).
2. In a non-stick pan, cook the bacon until crispy. Remove from the pan and set aside but retain the bacon drippings. In the same pan, sauté the onion, bell pepper, tomatoes, tomato paste, and rice.
3. Season with salt and pepper to taste. Add the water or chicken stock and bring to a boil. Cover the pan and place it in the oven for 30 minutes.
4. Remove from the oven and fluff the rice. Add the bacon pieces. Serve when ready.

Nutrition (per serving)
Calories 322, fat 12 g, carbs 45 g, sugar 4 g,
Protein 8 g, sodium 198 mg

DESSERTS

Jamaican Toto

This vegetarian dessert is the Caribbean's favorite coconut cake.

Serves 12 | Prep. time 10 minutes | Cooking time 40 minutes

Ingredients
½ cup butter, cut into small cubes
½ cup brown sugar
½ cup white sugar
2 eggs
1 teaspoon vanilla extract
3 cups all-purpose flour

3 teaspoons baking powder
1 teaspoon cinnamon
½ teaspoon salt
¼ teaspoon nutmeg
1½ cups evaporated milk
½ cup coconut milk
2 cups grated coconut

Directions

1. Preheat the oven to 375°F (191°C). Grease an 8x12 baking dish or pan.
2. In a bowl, cream the butter and sugars and add the eggs and vanilla. Beat everything together.
3. In a separate bowl, mix the flour, baking powder, cinnamon, salt, and nutmeg. Gradually add this to the butter mixture. Add the evaporated milk and coconut milk slowly until combined.
4. Add the grated coconut and pour the mixture into the baking pan. Bake for 40 to 45 minutes or until a toothpick inserted into the center comes out clean and dry.
5. Allow for it to cool on a cooling rack before serving.

Nutrition (per serving)
Calories 282, fat 7 g, carbs 47 g, sugar 21 g,
Protein 7 g, sodium 207 mg

Caribbean Bread Pudding

The bread pudding of the Caribbean islands with a touch of pineapple and apple and a rich rum sauce, it's delightful!

Serves 10 | Prep. time 20 minutes | Cooking time 45 minutes

Ingredients
2 cans evaporated milk
6 eggs, beaten
½ cup rum, divided
1 loaf day-old bread, cubed
1 can crushed pineapple, drained
1 large apple, peeled and grated
1½ cups white sugar
½ cup raisins

1 teaspoon vanilla extract
½ teaspoon salt
½ cup butter, cut into small cubes

Sauce
1 ¼ cup caramel sauce
¼ cup rum
Pinch salt

Directions

1. Preheat the oven to 350°F (177°C).
2. In a large bowl, whisk the evaporated milk, eggs, and rum until fully combined.
3. Toss in the bread cubes and stir to coat evenly. Blend in the pineapple, apple, sugar, raisins, vanilla extract, and salt.
4. Add the butter and blend well. Pour mixture in a greased 9x13 baking dish.
5. Bake for 45 minutes until the surface is golden brown.
6. To make the sauce, in a small saucepan, warm the caramel sauce over low heat. Whisk in the rum and salt and stir for 4-5 minutes until the sauce is warm. Remove from heat and set aside.
7. Allow for it to cool before serving with the sauce. Serve when ready.

Nutrition (per serving)
Calories 622, fat 23 g, carbs 96 g, sugar 75 g,
Protein 13 g, sodium 202 mg

Coconut Souffle with Rum

This deliciously decadent Caribbean dessert is made with shredded, sweet coconut, and rum.

Serves 8 | Prep. time 15 minutes | Cooking time 30 minutes

Ingredients
½ cup sugar, divided
1½ cups whole milk
2 tablespoons butter, unsalted
2 tablespoons vegetable oil
½ cup all-purpose flour
4 egg yolks
1 cup grated coconut
2 teaspoons coconut extract

¼ cup rum
8 egg whites
½ teaspoon salt

Directions

1. Preheat the oven to 375°F. Grease 8 ramekins with nonstick cooking spray and sprinkle sugar around the insides. Tap out excess sugar and assemble the ramekins on a baking sheet.
2. In a saucepan over medium heat, pour the milk. Once it starts to simmer, add the butter and oil. Blend in flour and cook, stirring constantly, until it forms a thick batter. Carefully pour in a heatproof bowl and whisk in the egg yolks, one at a time. Add the coconut, coconut extract, and rum.
3. Using an electric mixer, beat the egg whites and add the salt. Gradually increase the speed to high until the egg whites form stiff peaks. Stir one-third of the stiffened egg whites into the egg yolk mixture and gently fold it in. Repeat with the same with the remaining whites.
4. Transfer the batter to the prepared ramekins. Bake for 25 minutes until the souffle puffs up and is firm on the surface.

Nutrition (per serving)
Calories 260, fat 13 g, carbs 28 g, sugar 25 g,
Protein 7 g, sodium 235 mg

Poached Pawpaw

A light dessert made of papaya, perfect to finish any Caribbean meal.

Serves 4 | Prep. time 10 minutes | Cooking time 30 minutes

Ingredients
2 cups water
1 cup white sugar
2 medium-sized papayas, cut into ½-inch wedges
2 tablespoons fresh lime juice
Zest of 1 lime
1 cinnamon stick

Directions

1. Using a heavy-bottomed saucepan, boil the water and add the sugar. Stir until dissolved and the syrup starts to thicken.
2. Add the papaya, lime juice, zest, and cinnamon stick. Reduce heat and put to a simmer. Cook for 15 minutes.
3. Transfer the papaya to a serving bowl and continue boiling the syrup until it is reduced to 1 cup. Remove the cinnamon stick.
4. Allow the syrup to cool slightly and pour over the papayas.

Nutrition (per serving)
Calories 198, fat 0 g, carbs 53 g, sugar 39 g,
Protein 1 g, sodium 22 mg

Hummingbird Cake

The hummingbird cake originated from Jamaica where it was named the doctor bird cake, a hummingbird native from Jamaica. The cake has been popular ever since, especially in the Southern States of America. It boasts tropical flavors of pineapple, bananas, pecans, cinnamon, and nutmeg.

Serves 16 | Prep. time 35 minutes | Cooking time 40 minutes

Ingredients
<u>Dry ingredients</u>
2 cups all-purpose flour
1 teaspoon baking soda
1 teaspoon ground cinnamon

¼ teaspoon ground nutmeg
½ teaspoon salt
¾ cup granulated sugar
¾ cup packed light-brown sugar
1 cup pecans, chopped

Wet ingredients
3 large eggs
1 cup vegetable oil or canola oil
1 teaspoon vanilla extract
1 ½ cups mashed overripe bananas
1 cup fresh pineapple thinly diced or drained canned pineapple tidbits

Frosting
12 ounces cream cheese, nearly at room temperature
¾ cup unsalted butter, nearly at room temperature
4 cups powdered sugar, divided
1 ½ teaspoons pure vanilla extract
Pecans for decoration (optional)

Directions

1. Preheat oven to 350°F (177°C).
2. Lightly grease the bottom of 2 (9-inch) cakes pans and line the bottom with parchment paper. Grease the sides and bottoms with butter or cooking spray and sprinkle with flour taking time to turn the pans over remove excess flour.
3. In a large bowl, add all the dry ingredients and stir to combine well. Set aside.
4. In the bowl of the electric mixer, beat the wet ingredients EXCEPT the eggs.
5. In 3 batches, add the flour mixture, beat on slow speed until well incorporated. Add 1 egg and beat until well

incorporated. Continue with the same process until all the eggs are used. Continue beating for 1 minute on medium speed and cake batter is smooth.
6. Pour the batter evenly between the 2 cake pans.
7. Bake for 35-40 minutes or until a toothpick inserted in the center comes out clean.
8. Let the cakes pan rest on a wired rack to cool. After 15 minutes, loosen the sides of the cakes with a knife and unmold the cakes on the wired rack. Let cool completely before frosting.
9. While the cakes are baking, make the frosting. Beat the cream cheese and butter until creamy on medium speed. Working in batches, add 1 cup of the powdered sugar and beat until well incorporated. Add the vanilla and beat until well incorporated and frosting is fluffy.
10. Once the cake has cooled completely, frost the bottom cake, place second cake on top and finish frosting the cake.
11. Decorate with pecans if desired.

Nutrition (per serving)
Calories 641, fat 37 g, carbs 75 g, sugar 53 g,
Protein 6 g, sodium 176 mg

Spiced Chocolate Mousse

A velvety mousse with yogurt and cream everyone would certainly love.

Serves 10 | Prep. time 20 minutes
Refrigeration time 3 hours | Cooking time 30 minutes

Ingredients
1 cup heavy whipping cream
1 cup Greek yogurt, whole milk
3 tablespoons maple syrup
½ cup dark chocolate
1 teaspoon cinnamon
½ teaspoon allspice

⅛ teaspoon nutmeg
¼ teaspoon salt
⅛ teaspoon cayenne pepper

For the whipped cream topping
⅔ cup heavy whipping cream
1 tablespoon Greek yogurt
1 tablespoon honey

Directions

1. In a stand mixer, whisk the heavy cream to soft peaks. Add the Greek yogurt and maple syrup and mix evenly.
2. Using a double boiler, melt chocolate while stirring constantly. Remove from the heat and add all the spices. Cool and gently fold it into the heavy cream mixture. Transfer to ramekins and refrigerate for at least 3 hours.
3. For the whipped cream topping, whisk the heavy cream to soft peaks and add yogurt and honey. Serve this on top of the mousse while serving.

Nutrition (per serving)
Calories 371, fat 31 g, carbs 20 g, sugar 15 g,
Protein 5 g, Sodium 114 mg

Salted Caramel Tamarind Ice Cream

This refreshing tropical tamarind in salted caramel ice cream dessert would be the perfect way to end a meal.

Serves 4 | Prep. time 7 minutes | Cooking time 15 minutes

Ingredients
1 can coconut milk
½ cup tamarind purée
½ cup white sugar
¼ cup salted caramel syrup

Directions

1. In a saucepan, blend all ingredients and bring to a boil. Reduce heat and simmer for 10 minutes. Cool to room temperature.
2. Refrigerate for at least 1 hour.
3. Pour the mixture into an ice cream maker. Freeze according to the manufacturer's directions.
4. Serve with fruit on the side.

Nutrition (per serving)
Calories 442, fat 20 g, carbs 53 g, sugar 45 g,
Protein 5 g, sodium 173 mg

Gizzada

A classic Jamaican treat with a coconut tart with a shortbread crust.

Serves 8 | Prep. time 20 minutes | Cooking time 60 minutes

Ingredients
<u>For the crust</u>
2 cups all-purpose flour
½ cup butter, salted, cut into small cubes
½ cup very cold water

<u>Gizzada filling</u>
2 cups shredded coconut or desiccated coconut
1 teaspoon grated fresh ginger
2 cups brown sugar

1 teaspoon nutmeg
1 teaspoon allspice
½ tablespoon cinnamon
2 tablespoons vanilla extract

Directions

1. For the dough, in a mixing bowl, add flour and cut in butter mixture until it resembles coarse crumbs. Gradually add cold water and knead until it becomes a dough. Cover with a cling wrap and refrigerate for 20 minutes.
2. For the filling, in a bowl, combine the shredded coconut, ginger, brown sugar, nutmeg, allspice, cinnamon, and vanilla extract.
3. Boil a cup of water in a cooking pot. Pour in the coconut mixture and reduce the heat to a simmer. Cook until all the liquid has been absorbed. Set aside to cool.
4. Preheat the oven to 350°F (177°C) and prepare a baking sheet by lining it with parchment paper.
5. Cut the dough in 8 equal portions and roll it to about a 5-inch diameter. Pinch around the edges to form tart shapes and use a fork to prick the base of each cup. Prebake for 5 minutes. Remove from the oven and brush with beaten eggs.
6. Transfer spoonfuls of coconut filling into each of the tarts and return to the oven to bake for another 20 minutes or until the shells are golden brown.
7. Allow for it to cool before serving.

Nutrition (per serving)
Calories 438, fat 11 g, carbs 82 g, sugar 3 g,
Protein 4 g, sodium 10 mg

Bulla Cakes

A bread-like sweet dessert popular in Jamaica and well-loved by kids.

Serves 6 | Prep. time 20 minutes | Cooking time 30 minutes

Ingredients
2 cups all-purpose flour
1 cup muscovado sugar
1 tablespoon baking powder
1 teaspoon cinnamon
½ teaspoon nutmeg
½ teaspoon allspice
½ teaspoon salt
½ cup water
¼ cup melted butter
1 tablespoon honey
1 tablespoon ground flaxseeds
1 teaspoon vanilla extract
1 tablespoon grated fresh ginger

Directions

1. Preheat the oven to 350°F (177°C) and line a baking sheet with parchment paper.
2. In a large mixing bowl, mix all the dry ingredients. Blend evenly and set aside.
3. In a separate bowl, combine water, melted butter, honey, flaxseeds, vanilla, and ginger. Blend evenly. Add this to the flour mixture and mix until it forms a dough.
4. Knead for 3 minutes. Add flour if the dough is too sticky.
5. Roll the dough to about ¼-inch thick and use a cookie cutter to cut the dough to round shapes. Transfer the cookies to the prepared baking sheet.

6. Bake for 30 minutes or until golden brown. Serve when ready.

Nutrition (per serving)
Calories 345, fat 8 g, carbs 64 g, sugar 12 g,
Protein 4 g, Sodium 445 mg

Printed in Great Britain
by Amazon